My Design in Progress

My Design in Progress

a journal to unleash your imagination

ZONDERVAN®

ZONDERVAN

My Design in Progress

Copyright © 2020 by Zondervan

Requests for information should be addressed to:

Zondervan, *3900 Sparks Dr. SE, Grand Rapids, Michigan 49546*

ISBN 978-0-310-77069-5

Cover Design: Cindy Davis

Interior Design: Denise Froehlich

Contributor: Estee Zandee

Printed in Malaysia

20 21 22 23 24 / IMG / 10 9 8 7 6 5 4 3 2 1

INTRODUCTION

Creativity and design are some of the few things that can make a day brighter and lift our mood. And when the list of things we *have* to do continues to grow, art provides the chance to pause, reflect, express our thoughts and feelings, and, ultimately, savor and celebrate life.

Whether you're a master artist or this is the very first art journal you've picked up, consider this is your invitation to say hello to creativity and invite it into your daily life.

Much like creativity itself, this book doesn't have many rules. It doesn't matter where you start or how you progress. Draw, doodle, and paint all over the pages as much or as little as you like. Tailor these prompts to whatever works best for you. And remember, this book isn't about trying to draw or paint things just right or doing each activity perfectly. It's instead about sparking imagination in ordinary moments and finding inspiration in the unexpected.

All we ask is that you approach each page with earnest fun—a mix of taking each page seriously enough to do the activities and a flare of curiosity and adventure that results in time well spent.

Let's get started!

Hello, My Name Is...

> "Naming is one of the
> impulses behind all art."

MADELEINE L'ENGLE

Write your name in as many fonts and styles as you can. For example, draw it backward, upside down, highlighted, and in ALL CAPS. And don't forget to include your signature autograph!

Portrait Overlap

The search for creativity doesn't need to go any further than the end of your own nose. Grab the drawing tool of your choice in three or four different colors, as well as a mirror (or open your smartphone's camera and take a quick selfie—just no retouching!). Now select your first color and sketch your portrait by only looking at your reflection—in other words, keep your eyes more on your mirror image/selfie than on your paper. Draw fast and have fun. Then switch colors and draw another quick portrait right on top of the previous one. Repeat for the rest of the colors. Then sit back and enjoy how the sketches come together to create a master portrait.

> *"Painting is self-discovery. Every good artist paints what he is."*
>
> JACKSON POLLOCK

HaPPy DooDLes

"Happiness is a gift and the trick is not to expect it, but to delight in it when it comes."

CHARLES DICKENS

Fill this page with doodles of all the things that fill your little heart with happiness.

Color Splash

"It's not what you look at that matters, it's what you see."

HENRY DAVID THOREAU

Grab some paint (tip: watercolor might be risky, as it could bleed through the page) and make haphazard splashes and lines on the blank space below. Wait a few seconds for the paint to dry and see what images emerge. Maybe one brushstroke looks like a wave, maybe you see a forest of fuzzy trees or even a silly pet. With your favorite pen, doodle in the details to complete the collage of imaginative scenes.

MEMENTO

*"Nothing is ever really lost to us
as long as we remember it."*

L. M. MONTGOMERY

We all have belongings that are special to us—a stuffed animal from childhood, a keepsake or souvenir from a meaningful trip, a gift from a friend, or something passed down from a grandparent. In the space above, sketch an object that is meaningful and reflect on the good memories it holds for you.

Nature's Colors

Nature knows a thing or two about colors. In fact, the colors we use in our paintings and illustrations today originated one way or another from the earth. So experiment with the natural colors right in your own neighborhood. Run outside and gather any natural item that might make some color—things like flowers, pieces of bark, leaves, charcoal, dirt, berries . . . even chalky rocks can give some interesting hues when rubbed on paper. Then create a picture with the natural items you collected, or just have fun exploring the different-colored effects you can make.

In a Word

"Unique and different is the new generation of beautiful... You don't have to be like everybody else. In fact I don't think you should."

TAYLOR SWIFT

Fill this page with a dozen or so artful words that describe your personality. Try all different styles. We're talking bubble letters, calligraphy, modern, decorative, old-timey script . . . hand lettering galore! Throw in some shapes and numbers, fun colors and crazy patterns, doodles and smiles.

Rain, Rain, Don't Cause Me Pain

Even on the best of days, there's always something that seems to get us down and rain on our parade—harsh words, anxious thoughts, frustrating situations, and even actual rain. Label each raindrop with something that makes you feel a little overcast. Under the umbrella, write down the things that warm your heart and make you smile. When you're done, color in the umbrella with your favorite colors. Don't forget to take your umbrella of happiness with you wherever you go!

Portrait from the Future

"What will you do with your one wild and precious life?"

MARY OLIVER

You've magically received a snapshot of yourself—from the future! What do you look like, what clothes are you wearing, what task are you doing? From head to toe—and with all the detail your heart desires— draw or paint what you see.

In the Mood for a Landscape

"Be silent. That Heart speaks without tongue or lips."

RUMI

Sit for a moment and turn your attention to your heart. Imagine what your current emotions would look like as a landscape and illustrate it with your choice of art tools. Let your creativity run wild as you populate your landscape with nature-themed elements. Ask yourself things like: What would the weather be? What types of flowers and vegetation grow here? What animals might be hanging around?

Yum, Yum

"One cannot think well, love well, or sleep well when one has not dined well."

VIRGINIA WOOLF

Food has a special way of bringing us together and creating moments of community. Often the best meals are special simply because of the people we're with. Think about the most memorable meals you've had and illustrate one of your favorites. As you re-create the feast, think about what made it so special.

Family Tree

"Having somewhere to go is home, having someone to love is family. Having both is a blessing."

ANONYMOUS

Draw your family tree, starting with yourself and going back as far as you can. Illustrate each family member with a unique symbol, design, or mini portrait and add their name underneath. Don't forget to include yourself.

FULL CIRCLE

It's time for some stress-relief. Here's a no-pressure page to fill with circles: red circles, blue circles, small and big circles, spheres and ovals, bubbles and drops … whatever you feel like. Cover this page with all the circles you can design until no white space is left.

Coat of Arms

"Art, like morality, means drawing a line somewhere."

G. K. CHESTERTON

Each one of us lives by a code. Spoken or unspoken, we have a set of morals that are important to us and that we try to follow as much as we can. We might prioritize being kind and loyal, or fair, or telling the truth, or always giving our best. Take a second and identify three or four morals you live by and then design your own unique coat of arms.

Play the Hits

"Music is about imagination. It's about thought. It's about creating something from nothing."

Glenn Branca

Cue up your favorite song and hit play—be it an old tune that never gets old or your most recent love. Listen to it all the way through and let your imagination run wild. Then hit repeat and put what you see on paper. There are no rules here—be as abstract or detailed as you like, as monotone or vibrant as the song inspires you to be.

advertise this

Design an ad for an item you really love and use a lot—be it that classic T-shirt you pack for every summer vacation, your hands-down favorite pen, the pair of jeans that fit just right, or the water bottle that goes with you everywhere. In your ad, include a picture of the item and a few words describing what you love about it. The good news is, you don't have to make a purchase to enjoy this one—you already own it!

Figures in Motion

"The human body is the best work of art."

JESS C. SCOTT

Gesture drawings are very quick sketches of human movement and an energizing way to observe the rhythms and movements right in front of us. Go to a public place like a park or a restaurant, or simply turn on a show that has a few people you can sketch. Now watch (but try not to stare!), and when you see a gesture that interests you, sketch it as quickly as you can, focusing on the body's movement and not the details of the people themselves. Then move on to the next gesture until the blank space below is filled with a collection of messy sketches of the human body in motion. Remember, this is absolutely not about perfection but the simple practice of paying attention to the creative movement happening all around you.

Pattern Me Pretty

Fill each shape with a unique pattern. Try polka dots and stripes, solid colors and gradients, argyle and plaid, floral and geometric, as well as patterns of your own invention!

Picture of Kindness

"How beautiful a day can be when kindness touches it."

GEORGE ELLISTON

Sometimes the best art—the things most beautiful to us—are not hung in frames. Draw, paint, or write about something kind someone did for you—maybe it was a small gift, a comforting gesture, or an act of service. Now, that's something truly beautiful.

Health Check

"Balance is not something you find, it's something you create."

JANA KINGSFORD

It's time for a check-up. Consider how you're doing in each category and color in each column to the level that feels right. What area are you excited to see grow? Write down any ideas you have for making small changes toward filling it in even more.

Physical Well-Being

Mental Health

Relationships

Finances

Career

Fun & Creativity

Color Blend

"Art is a discovery of harmony, a vision of disparities reconciled, of shape beneath confusion."

ROBERT ADAMS

One of the greatest elements of art is that it can show how two seemingly opposing things are able to come together beautifully. For each panel, pick out two colors from the opposite ends of the color wheel. Fill in one end of the panel with the first color and the other end with the second color. Then blend the colors together in the middle. (Tip: It's easier to get a nice blend if you color in lightly at first and strengthen the color as you go.) Then sit back and enjoy this harmoniously colorful page.

TEXTURE CRAZE

"I search for the realness, the real feeling of a subject, all the texture around it ... I want to come alive with the object."

ANDREW WYETH

Let's go on a hunt for textures. Start with the items around you—a book with an embossed cover, a carved picture frame, a wooden surface, a raised pattern on a cup—or go outside and find leaves, bark, rocks, even the rough surface of the sidewalk.

Simply place the paper over the texture you want to capture and rub a crayon or colored pencil over the top to see a unique impression emerge. Fill the blank area below with fun textures and add notations about where each sample came from.

Dreamscape

"I dream my painting and I paint my dream."

VINCENT VAN GOGH

Our dreams are often the most creative work of our minds. Illustrate a recent dream you've had, complete with all the weird details you can remember. As you sketch, ask yourself whether you dreamt in color or black and white, what sensations you noticed, and what inspired the dream.

Mapmaker

"Anytime I feel lost, I pull out a map and stare.
I stare until I have reminded myself that life
is a giant adventure, so much to do, to see."

ANGELINA JOLIE

Pull out a "creativity compass" and design a map of a place you love,
or your neighborhood, or a place of your own imagining. Make sure to
include all the significant features, from nature to the human-made.
And like all good mapmakers, include creative names for each landmark.

Happy Place

What is your happy place—that comforting and inspiring location you go to in your mind, where you can feel safe and fully yourself? Maybe it's a memory from childhood or an imagined landscape made just for you. Inside the doorframe, draw and color your happy place. The best thing about a place like this is that the door is always open for you.

Monstrous Fears

"Our deepest fears are like dragons, guarding our deepest treasure."

RAINER MARIA RILKE

We all have fears that seem to puff anxiety and doubt into our lives. They steal pieces of our happiness and confidence. Underneath each scaly dragon, write down a fear that keeps you up at night. And remember, the funny thing about our fears is that they are usually guarding something special we don't want to lose. Give your worrisome fears a little love and understanding and color them in.

Color Exploration

"All colors are primary to my view of the world."

BOB BRENDLE

Pick three colors you dislike or don't normally gravitate toward. Now use them to sketch and color a simple nature scene. Explore how the shades look when overlapped and paired side by side.

TELL ME A STORY

At random, pick a type of animal, a place, and a thing. Better yet, have a friend or family member pick them for you. Then draw a picture with all three things (plus any others you want to add) in a way that tells a story.

Animal_____

Place_____

Thing_____

First Memory

"Memory is more indelible than ink."

ANITA LOOS

Our earliest memories often hold the essential parts of our personal stories. Think back to your very first memory—it might be very distinct, or it might be more of an impression. As you draw, paint, or write it, think about where you were when this memory took place, who you were with, and what you were thinking when it happened. Honor the little memory because whether sad or happy, distinct or vague, it no doubt played a role in who you are today.

MY FAVORITE T-SHIRT

Imagine a designer label gives you the opportunity to create a graphic T-shirt that is 100 percent you. What style, what colors, and what words and design would it have? Put it all together on the template here.

Gratitude

"Gratitude is happiness doubled by wonder."

G. K. CHESTERTON

Gratitude is a bit like magic. It has the amazing power to completely transform a humdrum day into a miracle. Populate this grid with mini sketches of things you're grateful for. And remember, gratitude is never wasted. There is nothing too big, too small, or too silly that we can't be grateful for it.

Pawfect Portrait

"Whoever said you can't buy happiness forgot little puppies."

GENE HILL

Pets. We have them or know someone who does. They're the adorable critters that make us feel loved, welcome us home, destroy our homework, shower us with kisses, communicate to us with a look, and add their own flair to our things with their shedding fur. Gather your favorite drawing tools and create a pet portrait of a furry or feathered friend, be it yours or your neighbors'.

Not a Pickup Line

Find an interesting view nearby—perhaps the local park or the view out your bedroom window. Grab a pen or pencil, settle into a comfortable position, and draw what you see. But there's a rule to this little exercise . . . once you put your pen down, you can't pick it back up. That's right; your entire drawing will be created from one long, continuous, uninterrupted line. (If you forget this rule once, it's okay: just put the pen back down where you last left off and continue on.)

PERSONALITY PLAY

There's always more to us than what meets the eye . . . and often more to us than we know ourselves. Think about the different roles and expressions of your identity you find yourself in most often—the focused self at work and school, the cozy and chill self at home with your pet, the chatty and funny self with friends . . . Now decorate each mask to match a role or expression of your identity. As you sketch and color, marvel at the creativity and vibrancy of your own personality.

And ... Action!

What is that one movie you're always down to watch again, or that show you can't seem to stop bingeing? It's time to give a little love to the entertainment that continues to enthrall you. Create your very own movie (or show) poster. Have fun with it—move your favorite character into the center even if they're not the main character and showcase your favorite quotes.

color Zen

They say coloring is one of the most calming activities you can do.
Fill in this entire page with your favorite colors and let your brain relax
and your thoughts wander. When you're done, consider what emotions,
ideas, or observations came to mind.

Botanical Study

"I thought I was pretty cool until I realized plants can eat sun and poop out air."

JIM BUGG

Tap into your inner scientist and forage outside for a handful of leaves, berries, and/or sticks. Draw them as realistically as you can, including all the details you notice. Then, like a real botanist, write down your observations for each item, such as your thoughts on the size, color, texture, as well as which plant it came from, and so on.

Group Portrait

"Many people will walk in and out of your life, but only true friends will leave footprints in your heart."

ELEANOR ROOSEVELT

No two relationships are alike; each one is unique. Find a photo of your close friends, family, or coworkers and re-create the image as a drawing or painting in the picture frame. For extra fun, give each person an accessory that match their personality. If you feel up to it, snap a pic of your awesome drawing and send it to your "models." And if you don't feel up to it, reach out anyway and tell your people you're thinking about them.

Creative Genius

"You are a creative genius. With more ideas than time, and more talent than utilized."

JENNIFER ALLWOOD

The funny thing about creativity is that it's rarely done on paper, because most creative endeavors are three-dimensional. Make a list of things you've created—from a batch of cookies to a playlist, a fun outfit for the day to a dinner party, a solution to a problem to a new friendship. Jot them down—or sketch out the activity, if you'd prefer—then appreciate what a creative genius you are!

All in the Angles

We go in and out of our
homes so much we hardly notice
their shape, colors, and size. Sketch or paint
your home from the front, from the back, what you imagine it
looks like to a bird flying above, as well as the view from a few yards down
the street. If possible, go outside for this exercise and enjoy the fresh air. Or
if the weather is nasty, finish these drawings as best you can from memory
and then step outside to check your work when the sun begins to shine.

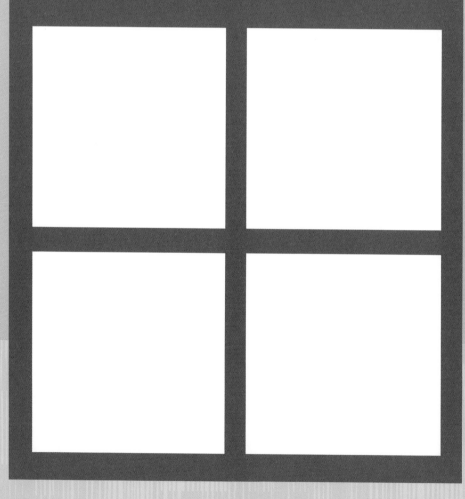

The Space Between

"The way you look at things is the most powerful force in shaping your life."

JOHN O'DONOHUE

We're far more used to looking and drawing the things that take up space, rather than the space around everything we see. But occasionally shifting our focus helps hone our spatial vision and make us better observers and artists. Set up a few interesting objects on a table or desk for a still life, and make sure the collection is spaced out a little. Pick up your pencil; though instead of drawing the objects, draw the negative spaces between and around each object. It will feel funny at first, but keep at it and enjoy the new perspective.

Changing Seasons

"The seasons are what a symphony
ought to be: four perfect movements
in harmony with each other."

ARTHUR RUBINSTEIN

Spring, fall, winter, summer—each season has its own kind of beauty. Sketch or paint an outdoor scene as it would look in each season. Note how the sun might be lower or higher in the sky depending on the time of year, and how the color palette changes.

Elements of Nature

"By discovering nature, you discover yourself."

MAXIME LAGACÉ

Wind, earth, fire, water, rock, wood, and metal: the mythic elements of nature. What is your favorite, the one you feel most inspired or intrigued by? Create a painting or drawing that reflects that element in a style as abstract or realistic as it makes you feel. As you work, think about why you relate to that particular element.

Role Model

"Each person must live their life as a role model for others."

ROSA PARKS

Who has been your role model? Someone who's helped you through a tough time, or guided and challenged you to be your best? Perhaps it is a teacher or coach, a parent or grandparent, a neighbor or a boss. Create a portrait of them or a picture showing how they helped you; you could also write a letter telling them thank you. As you work, ask yourself what you learned from them and what you want to teach others.

Stream of Consciousness

Let your mind wander and draw whatever thoughts come into your head. Maybe it's something from the past, the future, a to-do list, or the conversation you had last night. Let your thoughts set the pace and don't worry about fine-tuning each image—just follow your stream of consciousness on to the next thought and keep sketching until the page is filled.

Outside the Box

Ever feel like you've been put into a box? Sometimes the unkind or limiting words of others can make us feel boxed in, but most often we put ourselves in a box with our own fears, doubts, and worries about who we are and what we want to do with our lives. In each of the boxes below, write a limiting belief or phrase you've heard or that you tell yourself. Then fill the boxes with all the bright, happy color you can until you can only see positive vibes contained inside.

Cloudy with a Chance of Worry

"WORRY DOES NOT EMPTY TOMORROW OF ITS SORROW; it EMPTIES today Of its STRENGTH."

CORRIE TEN BOOM

Worries have a way of following us around and blocking out our personal sunshine like sad little clouds. The only way to dissipate them is to acknowledge why they are there. Inside the clouds, write or sketch your worries.

Now that you can see what's made your sky so gray, ask yourself what might be causing your worry. Is it desire for control, wanting to be liked, or an unmet need for rest? Is it concern and love for those around you? As you think about it, draw rainbows around and between your clouds as a way of chasing the gloom away. Then thank your worries for trying to help, but you've got it from here.

LOST AND FOUND

"What we have once enjoyed we can never lose; all that we deeply love becomes a part of us."

HELEN KELLER

Draw or paint something you lost—an old heirloom, a favorite book, or a toy that broke or disappeared one day, even a friend or family member who is no longer with you. Take your time and pour all your love onto the page. When you're done, give a little gratitude for the time you had and the memories shared.

Time Machine

Have you ever wondered what it would be like to live sometime in the past, within the world of a book or a show, or at some point far into the future? Create three self-portraits from three entirely different places and eras. Think about what clothes and hairstyle you might have, what objects might be included in the background, and how your posture might change for each one.

Shadow Art

Some of the best art integrates light and shadow—metaphorically and literally. Let's give it a try.

Turn on a desk lamp or find a place with strong lighting. Collect a few small items, such as a fork, a pair of scissors, a piece of fruit, a ribbon, or your glasses. Move the item around on the page until you get an interesting shadow. What does the shadow remind you of? Use your pen or pencil to "complete" the shadow drawing.

TIP:

Shadows have more clarity if the light source is angled from one side of the paper, rather than straight overhead.

TIME FOR VACATION

Sometimes you just need a mental break. Book an imaginary ticket to your ideal destination. Now paint or sketch your idea of the perfect vacation with all the rest, adventure, color, and texture you can imagine. Rip out the page and carry it with you so you can enjoy it whenever you need a mini vacation during your day.

"Let your imagination carry you anywhere that you want to be."

BOB ROSS

FANTASTICAL FAUNA

"Great things are done by a series of small things brought together."

VINCENT VAN GOGH

A myth about creativity is that it only creates brand-new things. But a lot of the time—including in great art—creativity connects things that already exist in new ways. Let's give it a go. With the art tools of your choice, create a brand-new, magical animal by combining the physical features of your favorite creatures. Don't forget to give your magical creation a name!

All About Perspective

The foundational challenge for all artists is creating depth and three-dimensional shape on a two-dimensional piece of paper. Good thing it's not as hard as it sounds. All it takes is a little shift in perspective.

Use the perspective lines to create a scene that shrinks into the point of distance. It can be anything you want—a cityscape, a landscape, a castle courtyard, or the space you're in right now. Whatever you choose, use the lines as your guides to make your buildings, rocks, trees, and people smaller in the background and larger in the foreground.

Simplify, Simplify

"Art is the expression of the profoundest thoughts in the simplest way."

ALBERT EINSTEIN

Art isn't only about what we put onto paper, but also about what we choose to leave out. Grab a pencil with a good eraser. Draw three quick sketches of objects immediately around you. Then take your eraser to each sketch and remove as many pencil marks as you can without losing the sketched object's overall shape. Feel free to go back in with your pencil and redefine the lines you want to keep. You might be surprised at how effective just a line or two can be.

Eyes Closed

"to draw, you must close your eyes and sing."

PABLO PICASSO

When we create, we combine two different parts of our being—the eye and the hand. The eye observes and measures while the hand uses muscle memory and intuitive instinct. Most of us rely on the eye, so this time, let's give the hand its chance to shine.

Pick something nearby to sketch. Study it for a full minute, taking in each detail and the overall shape and form. Then close your eyes—blindfold yourself if you need to—and let your hand show you what it remembers.

So Expressive

Humans have a lot of feelings, and most of us can't help showing them on our faces. Pick up your favorite pencil or pen, and in each box below, sketch a face with the corresponding expression. Make them as realistic or cartoony as you like. And feel free to grab a mirror and model the expressions for yourself.

Happy

Sad

Angry

Disgusted

Laughing

Mischievous

Scared

Bored

Amazed

A TIMELY CONVERSATION

Maybe you've heard the famous question: If you could have a conversation with anyone in history, who would it be? But instead of just writing down a name, take this question to the next level and paint or sketch your answer above. Whether you'd take a renowned artist to coffee, meet up with a legendary athlete, or share a meal with a family member, set the scene on paper and make sure to include yourself. As you work, think about what you would ask them and what you imagine they might say to you.

Feel free to reference photos of your historic figure to help inform your work, or let your imagination complete the picture.

LITTLE DISTRACTIONS

Chocolate chip cookies, shopping, that favorite show we can't stop watching—we all have guilty pleasures. Fill the chart with the activities you turn to when you need a distraction or a pick-me-up.

Most guilty pleasures are harmless activities that help us unwind and savor the good things in life. But an unhealthy habit can drain our energy and focus. Look over your list. What go-to activity needs to be replaced with a healthier option? What's one small step you can take today to start the switch?

Star Stuff

"The nitrogen in our DNA, the calcium in our teeth, the iron in our blood . . . were made in the interiors of collapsing stars. We are all made of star stuff."

CARL SAGAN

Amazingly, many elements that make up our world—and us!—are also inside the stars above us. So pull out all your colors and paints and create a galactic scene—stars, planets, asteroids, gaseous clouds, even black holes if you dare. As you work, think about how wonderful it is that materials from far-off places in our universe are at our fingertips every day.

Mini Goals

This is a fun-sized version of the five-year life plan. In the grid below, sketch or write goals you want to accomplish or begin in the next three months. Consider what small steps you can take to increase your personal growth and have more fun at work and school, at home, with your hobbies, with your health, and in your social life.

Something to Give

Creating art for ourselves is a beautiful practice, but art has always had profound meaning when shared with others. Color, composition, and linework combine to communicate feelings and passion, powerfully connecting the artist with the viewer, heart to heart.

Think of someone whose day could use a little brightening. Create a simple sketch or painting that they might make them smile or reach them in a special way. Then cut out the page and give it to them the next time you are together. And remember, it's not about perfection—it's about giving the gift of connection.

"Art is too important
not to share."

ROMERO BRITTO

Time Review

"The way we spend our time defines who we are."

JONATHAN ESTRIN

Time flies when we're having fun ... and when we're not paying attention. Take a second to reflect on where your time goes during your average week and then fill in the first pie chart. Use a different color for each focus and activity. Then fill in the second pie chart according to how you would *like* to spend your ideal week.

What is one adjustment you can make to your schedule today to move a little closer to your ideal week?

Color Moods

"Color is a power which directly influences the soul."

WASSILY KANDINSKY

Throughout history, people have used colors to symbolize specific emotions. Even today, we use colors very strategically to communicate our feelings. But sometimes the same color can call up a different emotion from person to person and culture to culture.

Create a simple landscape of your choosing, such as a desert, mountain range, jungle, farmland, cityscape, shoreline, or whatever inspires you. Quickly sketch the exact same landscape scene in each of the four frames below. Then pick a different color palette—with about three colors each—to match each mood description. Color in your drawings to see how color alone can evoke completely different feelings.

CALM, PEACEFUL, SOOTHING

ENERGETIC, VIBRANT, SATURATED

CONTRAST, STARK, SERIOUS

MYSTICAL, WISHFUL, DREAMY

Party Fail

"Failures are finger posts on the road to achievement."

CHARLES KETTERING

Most of us are very good about celebrating our successes and achievements, but not so good about celebrating our failures as well. The irony is our failures are the things that help us grow and learn the most; our failures equip us to do great things.

In the first column, make a list of things you've tried that backfired, fell apart, or could have been better. In the second column, write down something you learned from the experience.

Night Life

"I often think that the night is more alive and more richly colored than the day."

VINCENT VAN GOGH

There's something special and creative about the nighttime. After the day's tasks are done and the sun has set, the night offers us a sense of privacy and peace.

Draw or paint a night scene of your choosing. It can be an interior or exterior scene—anything from a city skyline lit up at midnight to the moon's reflection on water. Consider how the light is more nuanced and contrasted at night and the variety of color that becomes visible.

POINTILLISM

Pointillism is a fascinating art technique dating back to approximately 1886. Almost like magic, it creates a unique impression of all the colors of the rainbow with close-together, repeated dots of separate colors that the eye blends together. For instance, to create the illusion of green, an artist would pack tiny dots of yellow and blue closely together, and make purple with dots of red and blue or orange with dots of yellow and red. And in the end, the entire picture made of tiny dots looks like one big image with a lot of depth.

Grab your favorite markers, colored pencils, or paints, and using only the basic, "unblended" hues (red, yellow, and blue), color in the picture by using pointillism techniques and explore the wide variety of affects you can get with such a limited palette.

One Bold Line

"Drawing is taking a line for a walk."

PAUL KLEE

Draw a continuous line on the page; you can intentionally draw an object or portrait with a single, connected line, or simply go wherever your pencil wishes to move and create an artful doodle. Then go back and color in your new piece, and marvel at what you can create from a single flowing movement.

Dark and stormy

Think about a situation that darkened your day and brought on a tempestuous mood. In whatever style or medium you want, release those negative feelings and create a thunderstorm of color and lines on the page.

As the storm fades and your feelings calm, look for a silver lining, even the smallest one. Let it lead you to the sunshine.

Exploration Collage

"Creativity takes courage."

HENRI MATISSE

Creativity often sparks to life when we see colors, shapes, and lines intersecting in fascinating ways. Select a magazine or two, or a few old books and some scraps of paper. Then take out scissors and a glue stick (a thin layer of white glue or tape also works well). Cut out pieces from the magazines that catch your eye, arrange them in intriguing patterns, and glue them together. As you work, play around with contrast, shape, and color—try pairing things that you wouldn't normally put together and consider how you like or dislike it, and why.

Hall of Fame of Bad Ideas

"All good ideas start out as bad ideas, that's why it takes so long."

STEVEN SPIELBERG

We all have them: those ideas that sound good at first but turn out to be mistakes, comedic failures, or just plain silly. Some of those ideas are so epically bad that they are hall of fame–worthy. But even the worst ideas pave the way for better ones—sometimes in surprising ways. Create your own "hall of fame" by writing or illustrating your most notorious ideas inside the frames. Then under each frame, write what good idea or lesson came from that original bad idea.

What Does a Sense Look Like?

What's your hands-down favorite smell in all the world? How about your favorite sound? Taste and touch? Perhaps it's the smell of cut grass or your favorite perfume, the sound of rain on the window, a song from childhood, the taste of bacon in the morning or melt-in-your-mouth cinnamon rolls, the texture of a fuzzy blanket or a hug from someone you love. Whatever it is, try to translate each sense below into an artistic sketch or painting.

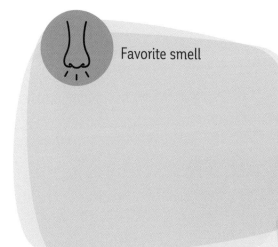 Favorite smell

 Favorite sound

 Favorite sense of touch

 Favorite taste

"You can find inspiration when you're not even looking for it."

JUDY WOODRUFF

There are times when you just need a little inspiration—a dash of motivation to get back to work, pick up that paintbrush, and try again with excellence. And the cool thing is, you probably have more sources of inspiration than you realize. It might be a catchy song, a role model, a friend who's always rooting for you, or a masterpiece that never ceases to stir your imagination. Write, sketch, or doodle your source(s) of inspiration below, and when you're finished, dog-ear this page so you can come back anytime you need a little recharge.

Bibbodi-boppodi-boo!

"it's not what you look at that matters, it's what you see."

HENRY DAVID THOREAU

For each of the unique shapes, work a little magic and transform them into a beautiful object or part of a scene. Draw outside the lines and be creative. It's okay if it doesn't work out perfectly. Have fun and try again.

To make the artwork even more meaningful, think about what thing in your life could use the same kind of transformational magic.

GET MESSY

This is a safe place to pick up your favorite art tools and go to town. Don't have a plan—just try things and see how it works out. Change things up halfway through. Flip the page upside down and keep working. Make a glorious mess. Life is messy, after all, but we can learn to see the beauty in it.

Flying High

"Far away there in the sunshine are my highest aspirations. I may not reach them, but I can look up and see their beauty, believe in them, and try to follow where they lead."

LOUISA MAY ALCOTT

Time to give your dreams some altitude. On each tail ribbon, write down a dream you have—big or small, realistic or out of this world. Let your imagination soar! Color in each kite and think about which dreams are keepers and which ones are simply pulling you off course. Circle or mark the dreams you want to let fly.

Behind the Name

Do you know the meaning of your name? If not, go online and learn how your name was derived and what it means. If your name is unique and doesn't have a common meaning, consider what inspired your caregivers to give you that name. Then paint or sketch a piece of art that reflects the meaning of your name.

INSPIRED GEOMETRY

"Geometry is the foundation of all painting."

ALBRECHT DÜRER

With either paints or pencils, create a design using geometric shapes. You may find it helpful to use a ruler or objects around the house as guides for curves and lines. Start out by making your design symmetrical, then suddenly make it asymmetrical. Now add a bright pop of color.

Finger Painting

"Every child is an artist. The problem is how to remain an artist once we grow up."

PABLO PICASSO

Connect with your inner child and rediscover the joy of finger painting. Pull out your (nontoxic) paints and water—and rags or paper towels!— and get to work. Experiment with colors, paint quantity, and pressure. Try using your fingernails for detail. But most of all, have fun.

Mug Love

Pour yourself a cup of relaxation and decorate these lovely mugs. Fill these vessels of happiness with your desired beverage, engrave them with sweet and witty sayings, or create the mugs you've always wanted to have, and let your worries fade away. Note: this activity is even more enjoyable when paired with an actual cup of your favorite hot drink.

SUPER YOU

"A superhero is any person really intent on making this a better place for all people."

MAYA ANGELOU

Nearly every one of us has imagined ourselves as a superhero at one point in our lives—be it someone with jaw-dropping powers or a person with amazing mental abilities that can outsmart any villain. Draw or paint yourself as that imagined alter ego. Don't forget to assign yourself a super name, a snazzy costume, and a signature, heroic stance. Comic books have nothing on you!

Mysterious Mysteries

"Without mysteries, life would be very dull indeed. What would be left to strive for if everything were known?"

CHARLES DE LINT

The world is full of lost things and fascinating mysteries—from Amelia Earhart's lost plane, Blackbeard's treasure, the ark of the covenant, the Bermuda Triangle, and Stonehenge . . . just to name a few famous ones. Maybe your family has a mystery of its own. Let your imagination solve a mystery, and sketch or paint a picture that shows what you think might have happened.

My Library

"I do believe something very magical can happen when you read a book."

J. K. ROWLING

From textbooks to fairy tales, biographies to comics, cookbooks to fantasies, books influence our lives in more ways than we can count. Inscribe these book spines with the titles of the books that shaped your life the most, letting the beautiful designs you create show your love for each story or lesson that affected you.

If you end up with a few spines without titles, write in a few titles you have always wanted to read.

Social Circles

We are more connected to each other than we realize. Write your name in the circle below, and then draw more circles floating around it that each hold the name of a relationship or social group you interact with—family members, classmates, coworkers, friends, clubs and teams, neighbors, your mail carrier, even the barista at your local café. Now draw colorful lines connecting each social circle to your name. As you build your social map, consider what your most important relationships need to help them grow.

Passion Project

"If you can't figure out your purpose, figure out your passion. For your passion will lead you right into your purpose."

T. D. JAKES

What thing spikes your interest and makes you excited? What do you love talking about, even with people who disagree with you? Maybe it's a thrilling sport, a global issue, a niche topic of knowledge, music, the arts, or being outdoors. Draw or paint a picture that shows your passion and why you love it so much.

ONCE UPON A TIME . . .

"Fairy tales are more than true: not because they tell us that dragons exist, but because they tell us that dragons can be beaten."

NEIL GAIMAN

From the tale of Cinderella to the adventures of Robin Hood, fairy tales and adventure stories have enchanted us since our childhood days. Pick your favorite fairy tale or adventure and the moment in the story you love the most. Then paint or draw your own rendition of that scene and swap yourself in as your favorite character.

Caffeinated Creativity

What could be better than the heavenly combination of sipping coffee and making art? Unless we're drinking coffee and making coffee art! Make a very, very strong cup of coffee, or tea if that's your beverage of choice. Experiment with the hues you can create by adding differing amounts of water and cream. Even smoosh the grounds (or tea leaves) onto the paper and see what happens. Then go all out and create a caffeine-inspired picture, or simply play with the different shades and shapes you can produce with your caffeine paint.

Free to Be You

We all have parts of ourselves we dislike, feel embarrassed about, or don't always know what to do with. For you, that might be a habit you can't kick, a tendency to easily become angry or feel hurt, or maybe a goofy side you'd rather keep hidden. Draw or paint a picture that represents this aspect of yourself. As you work, think about why this part of who you are makes you feel uncomfortable. Consider what it might look like to let your whole self come out and become fully you in all your uniqueness.

"Before you can be anything, you have to be yourself. That's the hardest thing to find."

E. L. KONIGSBURG

STAMPED

Make your own stamp using one of the options below, or come up with your own DIY idea. Once the stamp is ready, spread some paint onto a somewhat flat surface, like a plate, so you can easily dip your stamp, and fill the next page in a unique pattern.

Stamp-making ideas:

- Scratch or carve a symbol or lines into a bottle cork, an eraser, a carrot, or piece of apple or potato. (Tip: if you're using a fruit or veggie, pat it dry before dipping it into the paint)

- Wrap a piece of string or yarn around the end of a spoon or a piece of cardboard; dip the string-wrapped surface into your paint and stamp away.

- Crumple up some paper in a way that gives you some raised folds, and gently dip it into the paint and stamp lightly so the folds don't squish or flatten as you mark the page.

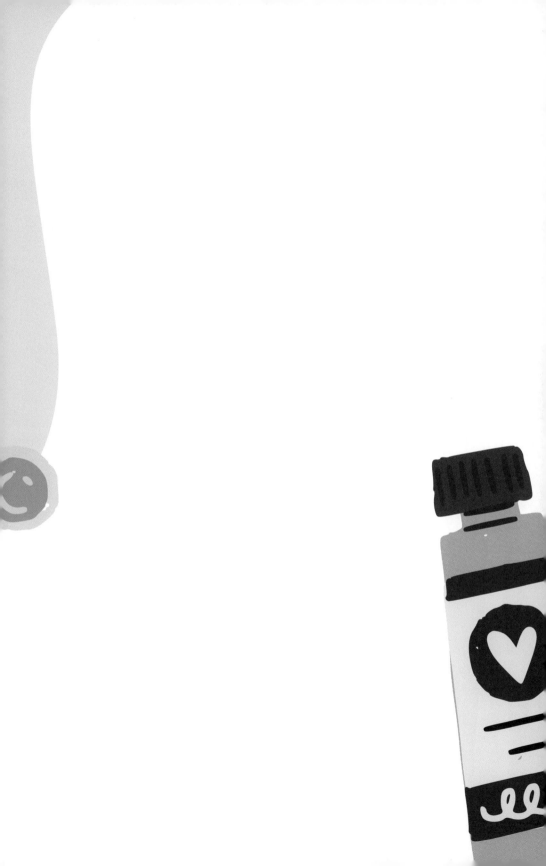

On the Other Hand

"When nothing goes right . . . go left!"

ANONYMOUS

Most of us have been taught to draw with one hand—our dominant hand. Years of practice form set patterns of thinking and drawing, which we don't even notice anymore because we're so used to them. But when we switch things up, we create new ways of seeing and moving, ways that let us explore shapes and lines and our own creativity in different ways.

Switch things up today by sketching your dominant hand (the hand you usually draw with) with your non-dominant hand. It may feel a little strange when you first begin using your hand and mind differently than you're used to. But enjoy the process and have fun thinking and moving in a new way.

GROW, BABY, GROW

"To plant a garden is to believe in tomorrow."

AUDREY HEPBURN

Look around and take in all the beautiful things growing in your life right now, from a buddying friendship to a developing skill to the actual plants in your house stretching their little fronds toward the sun. Top the roots with drawings of plants to signify each sign of your personal growth. Now just look at that bountiful garden!

As you sowed your garden, did you notice any plants that need a little pruning? What small act might you do today to help nurture their health?

"Life is either a daring adventure or nothing at all."

HELEN KELLER

What moments in your life got your heart pumping? Maybe it was scoring the winning point, a daring activity like zip-lining, or trying something new for the first time. Write or illustrate what gets your adrenaline rushing in the space below.

As you work, consider what was so thrilling about each activity and how can you build the emotions it spurred into your life more.

Here are some pages to play with your creativity: you can fill in the rest of a drawing or scene, make creatures out of random splats, doodle your thoughts, or use an image as inspiration. The important thing is to have fun!

"GET IN TOUCH WITH YOURSELF. THE FOUNTAIN OF CREATIVITY BEGINS WITH THE STREAM OF CONSCIOUS THOUGHT FLOWING INSIDE YOU."

NITA LELAND

"If you're always trying to be normal, you will never know how amazing you can be."

MAYA ANGELOU

"Art is not what you see, but what you make others see."

EDGAR DEGAS